HUTU
AND
TUTSI

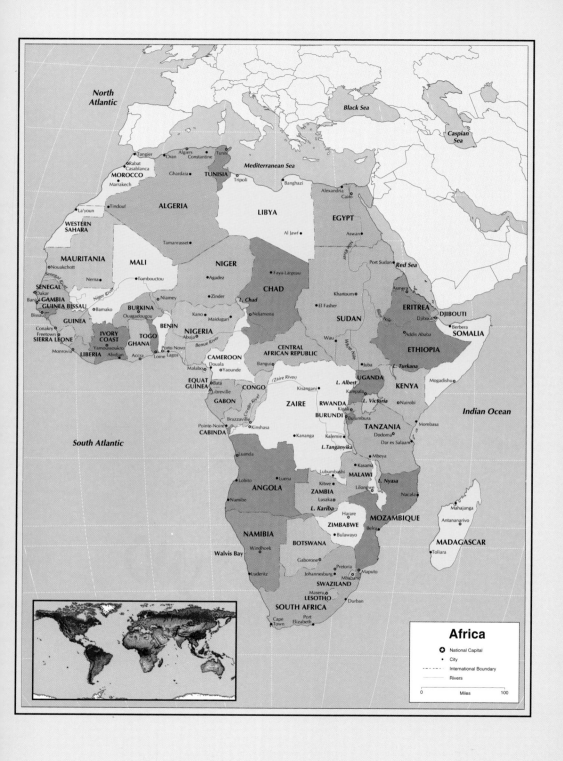

North
Atlantic

Black Sea

Caspian
Sea

Tangier
Algiers Tunis
Oran Constantine
Rabat
Casablanca
MOROCCO Ghardaia **TUNISIA**
Marrakech Tripoli Banghazi
Mediterranean Sea

Alexandria
La'youn Cairo

ALGERIA **LIBYA** **EGYPT**
Tindouf

**WESTERN
SAHARA** Al Jawf Aswan

Tamanrasset

Port Sudan **Red Sea**
MAURITANIA **MALI** **NIGER**
Nouakchott Asmera
Nema Tombouctou Agadez Faya-Largeau Khartoum **ERITREA**
SENEGAL Niamey **CHAD** Djibouti **DJIBOUTI**
Dakar Zinder El Fasher
Banjul **GAMBIA** Bamako Kano L. Chad Ndjamena Berbera
GUINEA BISSAU Ouagadougou Maiduguri **SUDAN** Addis Ababa **SOMALIA**
Bissau **BURKINA** Wau
GUINEA **BENIN** **NIGERIA** **ETHIOPIA**
Conakry **IVORY** Abuja Benue River White Nile **CENTRAL** L. Turkana
SIERRA LEONE COAST TOGO **AFRICAN REPUBLIC**
Freetown **GHANA** Porto Novo Bangui Juba Mogadishu
Monrovia Yamoussoukro Accra Lome Lagos **UGANDA** **KENYA**
LIBERIA Abidjan **CAMEROON** L. Albert **Indian Ocean**
Malabo Douala Kampala
EQUAT Bata Yaounde Kisangani L. Victoria
GUINEA Nairobi
Libreville **CONGO** (Zaire River) **RWANDA** Kigali Mombasa
GABON **ZAIRE** **BURUNDI** Bujumbura
South Atlantic Brazzaville **TANZANIA**
Pointe-Noire Kinshasa Kalemie Dodoma
CABINDA Kananga Dar es Salaam
L.Tanganyika
Luanda Mbeya
Lubumbashi Kasama
Luena **MALAWI**
Lobito Kitwe Lilongwe L. Nyasa Nacala
ANGOLA **ZAMBIA**
Namibe Lusaka Mahajanga
L. Kariba Harare Antananarivo
MOZAMBIQUE
ZIMBABWE Beira **MADAGASCAR**
Bulawayo
NAMIBIA **BOTSWANA** Toliara
Walvis Bay Windhoek
Gaborone Pretoria Maputo
Luderitz Johannesburg Mbabane
SWAZILAND
Maseru Durban
LESOTHO
SOUTH AFRICA
Cape Port
Town Elizabeth

Africa

✪ National Capital
• City
–·–·– International Boundary
——— Rivers

0   Miles   100

The Heritage Library of African Peoples

HUTU
AND
TUTSI

Aimable Twagilimana, Ph.D.

THE ROSEN PUBLISHING GROUP, INC.
NEW YORK

Published in 1998 by The Rosen Publishing Group, Inc.
29 East 21st Street, New York, New York 10010

First Edition

Library of Congress Cataloging-in-Publication Data

Twagilimana, Aimable
    Hutu and Tutsi/Aimable Twagilimana.
        p.   cm. — (The heritage library of African peoples)
    Includes bibliographical references and index.
    Summary: Surveys the culture, history, and contemporary life of the
two groups involved in the tragic civil war in Rwanda, the Hutu and the
Tutsi
    ISBN 0-8239-1999-4
    1. Hutu (African people)—Juvenile literature. 2.Tutsi (African
people)—Juvenile literature. 3. Rwanda—History—Civil War, 1994—
Juvenile literature. 4. Rwanda—History—Juvenile literature.
[1. Hutu (African people) 2. Tutsi (African people 3. Rwanda-History.]
I. Title. II.Series.
DT450.25.H86T93   1998
967.57104—dc21   97-27371
                             CIP
                             AC

Contents

Introduction   6

1. The Land and the People   9

2. The Arts   23

3. Religion   29

4. The Colonial Period   37

5. After Independence   44

6. The Future   57

Glossary   61

For Further Reading   62

Index   63

INTRODUCTION

THERE ARE MANY REASONS FOR US TO LEARN something about Africa and to understand its past and the way of life of its peoples. Africa is a rich continent that has for centuries provided the world with art, culture, labor, wealth, and natural resources. It has vast mineral deposits, fossil fuels, and commercial crops.

But perhaps most important is the fact that fossil evidence indicates that human beings originated in Africa. The earliest traces of human beings and their tools are almost 2 million years old. Their descendants have migrated throughout the world. To be human is to be of African descent.

The experiences of the peoples who stayed in Africa are as rich and as diverse as of those who established themselves elsewhere. This series of books describes their environment, their modes of subsistence, their relationships, and their customs and beliefs. The books present the variety of languages, histories, cultures, and religions that are found on the African continent. They show the historical links between African peoples and the way contemporary Africa has been affected by European colonial rule.

Africa is large, complex, and diverse. It spans an area of more than 11,700,000 square miles.

The United States, Europe, and India could fit easily into it. The sheer size is an indication of the continent's great variety in geography, terrain, climate, flora, fauna, peoples, languages, and cultures.

Much of contemporary Africa has been shaped by European colonial rule, industrialization, urbanization, and the demands of a world economic system. For more than seventy years, large regions of Africa were ruled by Great Britain, France, Belgium, Portugal, and Spain. African peoples from various ethnic, linguistic, and cultural backgrounds were brought together to form colonial states.

For decades Africans struggled to gain their independence. It was not until after World War II that the colonial territories became independent African states. Today almost all of Africa is ruled by Africans. Large numbers of Africans live in modern cities. Rural Africa is also being transformed, and yet its people still engage in many of their customs and beliefs.

Contemporary circumstances and natural events have not always been kind to ordinary Africans. Today, however, new popular social movements and technological innovations pose great promise for future development.

George C. Bond, Ph.D., Director
Institute of African Studies
Columbia University, New York

The Hutu and Tutsi are closely related peoples who live in Central Africa.
Although there has been a great deal of conflict between the two groups,
they share the same language and many other aspects of culture.
The man seen here is the leader of a band of drummers.

chapter

1

THE LAND AND THE PEOPLE

THE HUTU AND THE TUTSI LIVE MAINLY IN the central African countries of Rwanda and Burundi. These are the most crowded countries in Africa. Smaller numbers of Hutu and Tutsi are also found in the Democratic Republic of the Congo (formerly Zaire), Uganda, Tanzania, and in Europe and North America. Their total world population is approximately 14 million.

In Rwanda and Burundi, the Hutu make up about 85 percent of the population, while the Tutsi make up approximately 14 percent. The remaining 1 percent consists of the Twa people.

This book focuses on the Hutu and Tutsi of Rwanda, where the largest Tutsi population, numbering about 800,000, is found. The Hutu population in Rwanda is 7 million, and there is also a small Twa population. All three groups share the same national language (Kinyarwanda), the same culture, and the same religious beliefs.

The largest populations of Hutu and Tutsi live in Rwanda and Burundi. Many refugees from both groups have also fled into neighboring countries.

Although the Hutu and Tutsi live side by side throughout Rwanda, the Tutsi play a more prominent role in business and public affairs in Kigali—the capital—and in other cities. However, the Tutsi are also found in the more rural provinces, or prefectures, particularly in Gikongoro, Butare, and Kibungo.

The Hutu and Tutsi who live in countries other than Rwanda and Burundi are mostly refugees who have fled ethnic persecution. Conflict between the Hutu and Tutsi has been a problem in Rwanda since 1959. The more recent violence between the Tutsi and the Hutu in 1994 has been widely reported in the news. Although the troubles began in Rwanda, they spilled into Burundi, the Democratic Republic of Congo, Uganda, and Tanzania. The roots of these tragic events can be found in the history and culture of the Tutsi and Hutu.

▼ EARLY HISTORY OF RWANDA ▼

Little is known about the origins of the Tutsi, Hutu, and Twa. Experts agree that all three groups were already living together in the region of present-day Rwanda by about 900 AD.

The Twa were the earliest inhabitants of the region. Physically, they are very small. In the past the Twa lived by hunting and gathering wild foods.

The Hutu were the second to arrive; they

The Twa were the first inhabitants of Rwanda and Burundi. The Twa woman pictured above is making a clay pot.

When the Tutsi migrated to Rwanda with their herds of cattle, the Hutu were already established in the region on farms like the one seen above.

were farmers. They belong to the Bantu group of African peoples, which includes most of the peoples of central and southern Africa. The Tutsi were the last group to settle in Rwanda. They were nomadic cattle herders from northeast Africa.

Traveling in small groups, the first Tutsi to reach Rwanda were looking for fertile grazing land for their cattle. Tutsi warriors led the migration and protected the cattle herds against raiders. At first, the Tutsi had no single leader or political authority. A person's power within a Tutsi group was based instead on one's ancestry, intelligence, and courage.

At the time the Tutsi arrived in the region,

The livelihood of the Tutsi was based on cattle. When the Tutsi established the Kingdom of Rwanda, cattle became the key to status for both Hutu and Tutsi. The cattle seen above are being herded across the Ugandan border into Rwanda.

the Hutu were already living there in small, independent communities. The Hutu settlements were made up of clans, or people who shared the same ancestry.

Although the Tutsi were a far smaller group than the Hutu, the Tutsi took control over the Hutu, whom they regarded as inferior. By 1500 AD the Tutsi had established a kingdom called the Kingdom of Rwanda, which united the various small groups of Tutsi and Hutu in Rwanda.

▼ THE KINGDOM OF RWANDA ▼

The Tutsi, Hutu, and Twa all recognized the authority of the Tutsi king, or *umwami*. They believed that the *umwami* was sacred and divine,

THE DIVINE *UMWAMI*

The Tutsi held power in Rwanda partly because the Tutsi kings were seen as divine.

According to Tutsi oral literature, the king, or *umwami*, was the incarnation (the physical form of a spirit) of Imana (God). His subjects called him Nyagasani, meaning God or Lord.

The *umwami* was the source of the land's fertility and prosperity. All cows and women in the kingdom belonged to the *umwami*. He gave power and wealth generously, but could withdraw these privileges if he wished. He was the highest judge in the land. An *umwami* was regarded as perfect and beautiful even if he was physically unattractive. The *umwami* was immortal in the sense that his people would always remember him for his divine moral and physical perfection.

Because the *umwami* was regarded as divine, he was greatly respected. It was a religious offense to rebel against him or the kingdom. The *umwami* was the heart of the kingdom, and the kingdom could not exist without him. According to these beliefs, if the Hutu tried to revolt against the *umwami* and Tutsi control of the kingdom, they would suffer severe punishment at the hands of Imana and lose everything.

This and other myths served to discourage the Hutu from overthrowing the Tutsi monarchy.

owned everything in Rwanda, and controlled the fertility of the lands, herds, and people. They called him Nyagasani, the same name that Rwandan Christians use today to refer to God. They also identified him with the kingdom itself, hailing him as *U Rwanda rw'umwami*, which means Rwanda of the king.

The *umwami* was the supreme ruler of everything in the kingdom, including the court, the army, and the administration. He shared his power with his mother, who was known as the *umugabekazi*, or queen mother. The king was advised by a council of chiefs called the *abatware b'intebe*.

▼ THE *ABIRU* ▼

The secrets of the kingdom were kept by a council called the *abiru*. The *abiru* ensured that the king followed the rules of the kingdom. The king entrusted to the *abiru* the name of the son he wanted to succeed him. After the king died, the *abiru* announced which son would take the throne. If the *umwami* died unexpectedly without naming his heir, the *abiru* would choose the new king. If the *umwami* had no son, one of his brothers or half brothers would inherit the throne.

Appointing the new king sometimes caused disputes in the kingdom. One well-known example from Rwandan history is the Coup (or revolt) of Rucunshu, which occurred in 1896. When King Rwabugiri died, the *abiru* named his son Rutarindwa as his successor. However, Musinga, one of the king's sons by another wife, also claimed the throne. He staged a coup and defeated Rutarindwa's supporters. Rutarindwa

In the Kingdom of Rwanda the Tutsi required the Hutu to provide them with food products, such as the flour that the women (above) are seen selling at a market.

deliberately set fire to his own palace at Rucunshu and burned to death with his wife and three children. Musinga of the Bega was declared king.

▼ SOCIETY IN THE ▼
KINGDOM OF RWANDA

Status in the Kingdom of Rwanda was based on the ownership of cattle. In order for a Hutu to acquire cattle, it was necessary for him to work for a Tutsi family for several years. At the same time, the Tutsi required the Hutu to provide services for them and give them farming products. These factors placed the Hutu at a great economic disadvantage and pushed them into a lower class of society.

THE COW

The Tutsi first brought cattle to Rwanda. Since then, the cow has occupied a privileged place in society.

The cow was the focus of *ubuhake*, the Rwandan feudal system. The *garagu* (servant or vassal), lived with the hope that he would receive a cow from his *shebuja*, or feudal lord. After receiving the cow, the *garagu* swore an oath on the name of his *shebuja* by saying *yampaye inka kanaka*, which means "that person gave me a cow."

When the Rwandan feudal system ended in the 1950s, people continued to give cows as tokens of friendship or appreciation. Even today people continue to swear by the names of those who have given them cows: parents, brothers, or friends. It has become such an important custom that people often use the expression *yampaye inka data* to express joy, anger, or warning.

Now—as was true in the past—the cow plays a central role in marriage. The groom's family normally gives a cow to the bride's family. During the *gusaba* ceremony, the groom's family asks for the bride's hand in marriage. The bride is called Mutumwinka, meaning "you are asked to bring a cow," by her family. The cow symbolizes the union between the two families.

Giving a cow can create an unbreakable bond between any two people. A special ceremony called *gutanga inka* (meaning to give a cow) is held to celebrate the transaction. Both parties invite their families and friends to share a big feast. When the cow given at *gutanga inka* gives birth, the receiver gives a calf back to the original giver. This gesture is called *kwitura*, meaning to give back as a sign of gratefulness.

MILK AND HONEY

Because of the importance of the cow in Rwandan society, people associate milk, or *amata*, with happiness and heaven.

The Tutsi believed that eating should be a very private matter, because when humans ate food, they revealed that they were no different from animals. They preferred to consume only milk and other beverages, particularly banana wine, or *urwagwa*, and fermented honey called *ubuki*. *Ubuki,* which has an alcohol content of about 12 percent, was the favorite drink of wealthy Tutsi and Hutu and was therefore associated with prestige.

Milk and honey are still regarded as heavenly foods. This is expressed in the New Year's greeting used by all three ethnic groups in Rwanda: *Uzagire umwaka w'amata n'ubuki,* meaning to have a year of milk and honey.

An important part of a Rwandan wedding ceremony is the tradition of sharing a drink from the same container.

Some historians believe that only Tutsi were allowed to be warriors or hold positions of power in the kingdom. Other historians, however, point out that by the 1800s many of the great army commanders, or *abatware*, of the kingdom were Hutu.

The Tutsi upper class enjoyed many privileges, but the rest of the Tutsi were considered commoners like the Hutu. The Tutsi elite established a feudal system called *ubuhake*. A person of lower status (usually a Hutu) worked for a person of higher status (usually a Tutsi) in return for protection and some rewards, including cattle.

The two key roles in the Rwandan feudal system were *shebuja* (lord) and *garagu* (servant or vassal). In general, to be a rich lord meant that one was Tutsi, and being poor meant being a Hutu. This feudal structure gave military power and land to the Tutsi and to the very few Hutu who managed to acquire wealth and cattle. A few fortunate Hutu who were in favor with the rulers became Tutsi. This process of becoming Tutsi was called *guhutura*, meaning to shed Hutu status. Likewise, a Tutsi who lost land and cattle lost his rank and became a Hutu.

Intermarriage was quite common in the south of Rwanda, more often between Hutu men and Tutsi women than between Tutsi men and Hutu women. The children of mixed marriages adopted

In the late 1800s the difference between the Hutu and the Tutsi was more one of wealth and status than of ethnic background. A person who attained wealth could become a Tutsi. Therefore a woman such as the one seen here could be a member of either ethnic group.

the ethnic identity of their fathers. However, in
the northern areas of Rwanda intermarriage was
(and still is) discouraged.

By the time European colonists arrived in
Rwanda in the late 1890s, the labels "Tutsi" and
"Hutu" described a person's social status or class,
rather than his or her ethnic group. Status in the
Kingdom of Rwanda was fluid and flexible. A
person who was born Hutu could work to become
a Tutsi. The Twa, however, remained a marginal
group who were largely ignored by the others.

Under colonial rule the class differences
between Tutsi and Hutu came to be viewed more
and more as ethnic differences. Where a person's
status had once been flexible, it was now seen as
fixed at birth by the person's ethnic background.
This shift in viewpoint came about both because
of Europeans' ideas about race and ethnicity and
because Hutu and Tutsi increasingly emphasized
their ethnicity. Later, ethnic differences led to
terrible violence between the two groups in
Rwanda, Burundi, and neighboring countries. ▲

2

THE ARTS

TUTSI ARTS, INCLUDING LITERATURE, MUSIC, and crafts, were strongly associated with the king's court. Because the king was regarded as sacred, these courtly arts can be considered religious. Artists often belonged to special guilds.

▼ COURT POETRY ▼

Court literature was mostly composed by Hutu poets who served the court. Ordinary Tutsi and Hutu sometimes learned court poems and then recited them to their own *shebuja*, or lord.

There were four main types of court poetry. The first type, *ibisigo*, used highly poetic language to praise the great deeds of Tutsi kings and heroes.

Ibyivugo, the second type, included conventional poems that praised the courage of warriors and the quality of their arrows, spears, and shields. Apart from learning these poems, every warrior also had to compose praise poems about himself, which he sang on the battlefield to frighten the enemy. During their military training, warriors organized contests of poetry and dancing, which were held at night.

The third type of court poetry was called *amazina y'inka*, meaning names of the cows. It consisted of poems praising the beauty and courage of the royal cattle, or *inyambo*, meaning the cattle with long horns. These poems usually described the herd as divided into two warring camps and praised the animals' beauty and courage as if they were warriors in the king's army.

Historical narratives, or *ibitekerezo*, were the fourth type and were an important source of Rwandan history. These poems were composed either in verse or in prose by special guilds of poets known as *ubucurabwenge*, which means creation of wisdom.

▼ DESIGN ▼

The first Europeans who visited Rwanda were very impressed with Tutsi designs, especially the beautiful patterns on baskets, pottery, and shields. Bold geometric designs, usually in black, red, or white, adorned these objects.

▼ ORAL LITERATURE ▼

Before writing was introduced, Hutu and Tutsi stories were passed from generation to generation by

Designs such as these are an important part of the artistic
heritage of the Tutsi.

word of mouth. Folktales, or *imigani,* were often recited. Characters in the tales include Imana (God), kings, heroes, spirits of heroic ancestors, ordinary people, natural elements, and animals.

Ibihozo, or consolation songs, were composed for newly married women to comfort them when they left their families' homes. Other popular forms were lullabies, proverbs, and riddles, or *ibisakuzo,* which are all still part of daily speech in Rwanda.

After Europeans introduced writing, anyone who could read or write had access to literature. In other words, literature became a popular means of expression that no longer had to focus on the court. It was no longer controlled by the guilds of poets who had mastered complicated, poetic, courtly language.

▼ MUSIC AND DANCE ▼

Drums, flutes, harps, and other small instruments were popular among both the Hutu and the Tutsi.

Drums were strongly associated with the court, where drummers entertained the royalty. Drums were also used to call people to public meetings. In many Rwandan schools today, drums are used instead of bells to signal the end of each class.

At their training camps, the *intore,* or warriors, practiced dances that imitated movements on the

SYMBOLS OF TUTSI AUTHORITY

The highest symbol of Tutsi royalty was the royal drum, or *karinga*. As sacred as the king himself, the *karinga* was surrounded by lesser drums and stored in a house where a sacred fire was kept burning. The drums were sprinkled with bull's blood to honor the drum and to enhance its power. The genitals of defeated enemies were attached to the *karinga*, which was therefore a symbol of Tutsi victory and superiority over others.

Like the *karinga*, court poetry also celebrated Tutsi rule and often justified or reinforced it. One example is the poem entitled Inganji Karinga, which means the triumphant *karinga*.

The poem states that the very first Rwandan was named Kigwa. He fell from heaven with his three sons: Gatwa, the ancestor of the Twa people; Gahutu, the ancestor of the Hutu people; and Gatutsi, the ancestor of the Tutsi.

When the time came for Kigwa to choose which of his sons should succeed him, he decided to test them. He gave each of them a pot of milk to watch over during the night. By daybreak, Gatwa had drunk all the milk in his pot. Gahutu had fallen asleep, knocked over his pot, and spilled the milk. Only Gatutsi had watched over his pot carefully throughout the night. This showed that only Gatutsi was responsible enough to rule. Kigwa made Gatutsi his successor and relieved him of menial tasks. Gahutu was to be his servant. Because Gatwa was completely unreliable, he could only be a clown in society.

Supporters of Tutsi rule in the 1950s used this story to justify the Tutsi's right to rule over others and their refusal to share power.

Drumming bands, such as the one seen here, often include as many as nine drums, each with a different pitch.

battlefield. The best dancers gave solo performances in front of the whole group. Drums, horns, and flutes accompanied the dances. Other people danced at social occasions, such as weddings, funerals, and community gatherings. People in the crowd clapped their hands to enhance the dancing rhythm.▲

chapter

3
RELIGION

BEFORE THE INTRODUCTION OF CHRISTIANITY in the early 1900s, the Tutsi, Hutu, and Twa followed their own religions.

▼ THE SUPREME BEING ▼

Before Europeans arrived, Rwandans believed in a Supreme Being called Imana. (Today Imana is identified with the Christian God.) Imana was also referred to by other names that praised his individual qualities. These names included Rugira, the Supreme; Rurema, the Creator; Iyakare, the One at the origin; and Rugaba, the Generous Provider.

Rwandans did not perform any special rites for Imana. However, they addressed Imana in their prayers and gave their children names that honored him. Examples of such names are Habimana, meaning god is supreme; Habarurema, meaning the Creator is supreme; Habiyakare, meaning the One at the origin is supreme; and Twagirimana, meaning only god can save us.

▼ CREATION ▼

In the minds of Rwandans, Imana created the first people. One Rwandan creation story states that Imana expelled the Tutsi from the divine world because of some mistake that their mother made. When the Tutsi arrived on earth, they found the Twa and the Hutu already living there.

Another version of the creation story says that Imana created the Hutu and the Twa on earth. Other stories say that all three ethnic groups in Rwanda all lived in heaven. There they were each given their traditional livelihood: the Tutsi learned cattle herding, the Hutu learned farming, and the Twa learned hunting.

▼ THE ANCESTORS ▼

In the past (and in many cases today) Rwandans believed that Imana was inherently good, needed nothing, and rarely intervened in people's lives. On the other hand, they believed that the spirits of ancestors, *abazimu*, lived in the underworld and frequently troubled humans.

The underworld was an unpleasant place, and the *abazimu* resented living there. They often left the underworld and caused confusion or sickness in the lives of the living. Some spirits were even

According to one version of the creation story that is told in Rwanda, the Hutu were given their farming livelihood by the Creator in heaven. Today Rwandan children of all ethnic groups learn farming techniques in school.

said to stay on earth in small huts built for them by their living family members.

To please and calm the *abazimu*, their living relatives had to worship them. The main way of doing this was to give them offerings. Offerings could be small, such as a few drops of milk or beer or some cooked beans thrown on the ground. On more important occasions, a larger offering was made by sacrificing a goat or bull. Such offerings were accompanied by praises sung to please the spirits, who can hear but not see.

Making offerings to the ancestors was usually the responsibility of the head of the family. To get rid of the worst spirits, however, a family would have to call in a religious specialist, or diviner. In some cases a diviner would instruct a young woman to sleep near the place occupied by a troubling spirit in order to calm that spirit.

▼ DIVINERS ▼

In traditional Rwandan society, a diviner, or *umupfumu*, was endowed with the power to divine, or interpret, the will of Imana and was therefore regarded as the son of God. Many Rwandans still consult diviners today.

A diviner generally specialized in one of several divination methods that were used to interpret the will of God. *Guhanura*, meaning to prophesy, was divination that used intuition and inspiration from the spiritual world. Another divination method was called *kuraguza inzuzi*, meaning divination using pieces of wood. This involved throwing small pieces of wood onto a flat surface and reading messages according to the way the pieces fell.

Kuraguza urugimbu, meaning divination using fat, involved reading messages from the fat or intestines of animals. Chickens could be sacrificed for this form of divination, or the diviner could use fat from previously slaughtered goats, sheep, or cattle. The diviner mixed the fat with herbs and let it dry. Then he placed it inside a pot, which was tilted toward him, and lit the fat like a candle. For several hours he would watch the flame to interpret its messages.

▼ THE HERO SPIRITS ▼

In traditional Rwandan religion, the spirits of dead heroes, or *imandwa*, are particularly powerful and require special worship.

The chief of the thirty or so *imandwa* is Ryangombe, who is said to have inherited his position from his father. Ryangombe and his own son fought off a challenge from another *imandwa* who wanted to become chief. Ryangombe's reign on earth was cut short by a mysterious event. While hunting, Ryangombe was attacked by a buffalo so unnaturally large that people suspected that spiritual forces were involved. The buffalo threw him against a tree. As he lay dying under the tree, Ryangombe declared that all Tutsi, Hutu, and Twa (except the king) should worship him as the king of the *imandwa* in a special ceremony called Kubandwa.

Another well-known *imandwa* is Nyabingi. Nyabingi was an unmarried woman who was murdered and made immortal by Imana. She is a rebellious spirit who is worshipped mainly by the Hutu in northern and northwestern Rwanda and in Uganda. Those who have opposed the authority of Tutsi rulers and of European colonial powers have often joined the Nyabingi cult.

Unlike Ryangombe, Nyabingi is served by priests and priestesses—also called Nyabingi— who stand between her and her worshippers. In

KUBANDWA

Kubandwa was a form of initiation during which young Hutu and Tutsi adults were brought under the spiritual protection of the *imandwa*. During the ceremony, previous graduates of Kubandwa served as role models for the initiates. Called cult fathers or cult mothers, they represented particular *imandwa*, whose behaviors and expressions were then imitated by the initiates. They taught the initiates the secret language used by graduates and songs honoring Ryangombe and other *imandwa*.

The initiates were painted in white clay, acted wildly, and called each other by the name Ryangombe. They were also beaten and made to swear against their mothers. These behaviors were all part of the process of growing up and adopting the examples set by past heroes. Initiates regularly drank a bitter, red drink. This was a symbol of blood, suggesting that the initiates shared the same blood and were now all part of a new "family" consisting of all adults.

At the final graduation ceremony, each initiate lay beside his or her cult mother or cult father for a few minutes, as if taking on their heroic qualities before entering a new life as an adult.

the past these priests have been able to use their positions politically to oppose the authority of the Tutsi and the Europeans. They also benefit by receiving sacrifices that worshippers give to them on behalf of Nyabingi. A family might, for example, honor Nyabingi by giving a young girl to a Nyabingi priestess as her servant.

▼ CHRISTIANITY ▼

The introduction of Christianity completely changed the religious practices of Rwandans. When asked to state their main religion in 1991, 62 percent of Rwandans reported themselves as Catholic, 18 percent as Protestant, 19 percent as followers of only traditional worship, and 1 percent as Muslim.

These statistics only tell part of the story. In fact, most people combine their traditional religion with Christianity or Islam. Both of these religions often discourage Rwandan traditional practices. In order to be baptized in the Rwandan Catholic church, for example, people must say that they reject traditional practices such as Kubandwa. Requiring converts to Christianity to reject Rwandan traditions has meant that many Rwandans, especially the young generation, have lost touch with their traditional beliefs.

During colonial times, more Tutsi than other groups entered Christian schools and joined the clergy. After independence in Rwanda in 1962, many Tutsi entered the clergy as a way to escape the ethnic discrimination they experienced in other jobs. Although the clergy became dominated by Tutsi, this did not discourage Hutu from joining.

The ethnic violence that broke out between Hutu and Tutsi in 1994 led many Rwandans and foreigners to declare that Christianity had failed in Rwanda. Thousands of Tutsi and Hutu were massacred inside churches, where they had taken refuge, believing that nobody would kill in a sacred place. Some Hutu priests, nuns, and pastors betrayed their Tutsi colleagues to killers or took part in the murders themselves.▲

4
THE COLONIAL PERIOD

AT THE END OF THE 1800S THE KINGDOM OF Rwanda was a powerful state in Central Africa. At this time European powers were competing with each other to establish colonies in Africa, a period known as the Scramble for Africa.

The first European explorers reached Rwanda while searching for the source of the Nile River. They described the Tutsi and Hutu of Rwanda and Burundi using racial terms to contrast the two groups.

▼ RACIAL STEREOTYPES ▼

The Europeans formed stereotypes, or oversimplified mental pictures, about the Hutu and Tutsi people. According to their descriptions, the Tutsi were tall and light skinned. The Tutsi were often said to be quiet, reserved, and relaxed. However, some Europeans

interpreted these same qualities negatively, saying that the Tutsi were secretive, arrogant, and lazy. Europeans also sometimes interpreted the Tutsi's wealth and power as the result of shrewd, opportunistic, or unscrupulous behavior on their part. Some Europeans even suggested that the Tutsi rarely spoke their mind and often lied, especially when dealing with strangers.

Nevertheless, during the early colonial period most Europeans believed that the Tutsi were natural born leaders. They saw the Tutsi as superior to the Hutu in all respects and believed that the Tutsi were therefore destined to rule the Hutu. Because many Tutsi were taller than the Hutu, Europeans thought that the Tutsi were nobler and more advanced than the Hutu. The Europeans believed that the Tutsi were descended from Ham, a person mentioned in the Bible, and called them Hamites.

In contrast, Europeans described the Hutu as shorter and darker than the Tutsi. According to Europeans, the Hutu were servile, rowdy, gluttonous, cowardly, and undignified.

All of these stereotypes resulted partly from racist ideas and theories that Europeans brought with them to Rwanda and partly from the attitude of many Tutsi who regarded themselves as superior to Hutu. Today we know that such racist ideas are false. The fact that the Tutsi were cattle herders who consumed high

During the colonial period, Europeans believed that the Tutsi were a superior people. Tutsi warriors, or *intore*, such as those pictured above, were regarded as belonging to a brave and noble race.

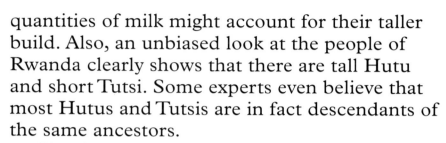

quantities of milk might account for their taller build. Also, an unbiased look at the people of Rwanda clearly shows that there are tall Hutu and short Tutsi. Some experts even believe that most Hutus and Tutsis are in fact descendants of the same ancestors.

Clearly the Europeans' views were not based on a close observation or a clear understanding of society in the Kingdom of Rwanda. Nevertheless, when Rwanda became a European colony, these European ideas began to shape events in Rwanda and have a strong influence on Rwandan society.

▼ COLONIAL OCCUPATION ▼

Rwanda first fell under the authority of Germany (1896-1916) and later under Belgium (1916-1962). These colonial governments followed a system called indirect rule. This means that they left existing African authorities in place and used them to carry out the Europeans' colonial policies.

Both the German and Belgian governments in Rwanda kept Tutsi authorities in power and supported them if they were ever challenged. In this way, the European colonial powers reinforced the existing social status and confirmed the biased view that the "intelligent, refined, and courageous" Tutsi were born to rule over the "cowardly and stupid" Hutu.

This photograph, taken during the colonial era, has been carefully posed to show several traditional occupations in a Tutsi village.

▼ THE END OF COLONIAL RULE ▼

During the colonial period, European missionaries set up schools in Rwanda where both Tutsi and Hutu children received formal Western education and Christian teachings. In the 1950s educated Africans throughout the continent (who were mostly trained at these and similar missionary schools) played a leading role in demanding their countries' independence from European colonial rule.

In Rwanda the desire for freedom and democracy led Hutu intellectuals to question both colonial control and the positions of privilege that the Tutsi held in colonial Rwanda. In 1957 a group of Hutu intellectuals published

41

the Bahutu Manifesto, which called for an end to
what they called Tutsi colonization. They wrote
that it was unjustifiable that the Tutsi, a mere 15
percent of the population, dominated every
aspect of Rwandan life, including the military
and the government. To bring about a more
democratic society, they demanded an end to the
feudal system of *ubuhake* and called for a fairer
system of sharing power. However, they did not
demand Rwanda's independence from Belgium.
The demands of the Bahutu Manifesto held
broad appeal for the Hutu population.

One year later a group of Tutsi intellectuals
and court members responded by issuing their
own document from Nyanza, the Tutsi royal
capital of Rwanda. This document stated that
the proper relationship between the Tutsi and
the Hutu was one of *shebuja* and *garagu*, of lord
and vassal, and that therefore the Hutu should
not expect to share power with the Tutsi. The
Tutsi began to demand Rwanda's independence
from Belgium.

These opposing documents hardened the
views of the more radical Tutsi and Hutu. At the
same time, the Belgian colonial government
began to shift its support from the Tutsi elite to
the Hutu, who demanded democracy but not
the end of Belgian control.

Tensions between the Tutsi and Hutu increased
and finally resulted in the Rwandan Revolution,

which overthrew the Tutsi. Violence broke out in November 1959. Thousands of Tutsi were killed and hundreds of thousands fled to neighboring countries, including the last Tutsi king, Kigeri V, also known as Kigeri V Ndahindurwa.

The Hutu victory was due both to their far larger numbers and the support they received from the Belgian colonial government. Many Tutsi believe that far fewer Tutsi would have died if the Belgian administration had stayed neutral.

On January 28, 1961, a congress of Hutu councillors and leaders, with the support of the Belgian administration, officially proclaimed the end of the Tutsi monarchy and the birth of the Republic of Rwanda. The new republic gained its independence from Belgium on July 1, 1962.▲

5
AFTER INDEPENDENCE

THE HUTU BECAME THE RULERS OF independent Rwanda, but between 1963 and 1967 the Tutsi in exile made at least a dozen attempts to retake power by force. The Hutu avenged these attacks from Tutsi in neighboring countries by attacking the Tutsi still living in Rwanda. Some of these revenge attacks were organized by the new Hutu rulers. Following a Tutsi raid on Rwanda in 1963, Hutu authorities in Gikongoro Prefecture organized the massacre of more than 10,000 Tutsi. These authorities were never brought to trial.

Violence also broke out in neighboring Burundi in 1965, where the Tutsi seized control of the government and the military there. They killed approximately 5,000 Hutu civilians who opposed them. In the early 1970s Hutu exiles living in Tanzania frequently attacked Burundi. It is estimated that the Tutsi government killed

Ethnic violence broke out between Hutu and Tutsi in the 1960s.
Thousands of each group were killed or became refugees like the
people seen in this photograph.

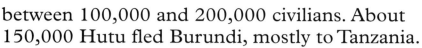

between 100,000 and 200,000 civilians. About 150,000 Hutu fled Burundi, mostly to Tanzania.

The Tutsi were often blamed for political problems in Rwanda in order to justify revenge attacks against them. In 1972 the Hutu-led military in Rwanda used the killing of Tutsi as part of their plan to overthrow the civilian Hutu government. The military killed hundreds of Tutsi to create the impression that the civilian government was not in control of the country. During the ethnic violence, the military successfully staged a coup, taking over and replacing the civilian government in 1973. Attacks against the Tutsi stopped immediately.

▼ LIFE UNDER RWANDA'S ▼ MILITARY GOVERNMENT

Both the Hutu civilian and military governments oppressed the Tutsi through direct attacks and through discrimination. In order to get an education, many Tutsi had to enroll in private schools, which were far more expensive than public schools. Many Tutsi changed their official ethnicity to Hutu in order to attend a public high school or university or to enjoy the other advantages of being Hutu under Hutu rule. The Tutsi were also excluded from important positions in the military and in the administration.

After the 1973 coup, the military president,

The ethnic identity of Rwandans was registered at birth on official identity documents. To avoid discrimination, many Tutsi changed their official ID cards to Hutu. When Tutsi were killed on the basis of their race, having a Hutu ID could mean the difference between life and death.

Major General Habyarimana, introduced a new policy. It claimed to share Rwanda's resources fairly among the country's different regions and ethnic groups. In reality, it discriminated against both the Tutsi and those Hutu who did not come from President Habyarimana's home region. As a result the Hutu military government was opposed by many Tutsi and by Hutu from the southern part of the country.

▼ REFUGEES ▼

As a result of the 1959 Rwandan Revolution, thousands of Tutsi had fled to neighboring countries. After the revolution died down, the Hutu governments (both civilian and military) tried to prevent the Tutsi refugees from returning to Rwanda. Many of these refugees ended up living in refugee camps for more than thirty years.

To fight the Hutu government of Rwanda, these Tutsi refugees formed the Rwandan Patriotic Front (RPF) in the 1980s. They assembled a powerful force of about 10,000 men. On October 1, 1990, the RPF attacked Rwanda from neighboring Uganda.

In response, the Rwandan government arrested more than 8,000 of its opponents in Rwanda, including both Tutsi and Hutu. These government opponents were held in terrible conditions for several months. They were accused of being *ibyitso*, meaning accomplices of the invaders.

During the next four years the RPF continued to launch attacks against Rwanda with increasing success.

▼ HUTU EXTREMISTS ▼

The RPF attacks against Rwanda enraged Hutu leaders in Habyarimana's government. They decided to take extreme steps to stamp out

The military government of President Habyarimana (above) was
dominated by Hutu from the president's home region. Tutsi refugees in
Uganda formed a guerrilla army, the Rwandan Patriotic Front (RPF), to
attack Rwanda and overthrow Habyarimana's government.

all opposition to the Rwandan government. These Hutu extremists planned to eliminate both Tutsi and Hutu who opposed the government of Rwanda. The Hutu extremists assembled hit lists of all government opponents.

Some Hutu extremists argued that the solution to Rwanda's problems was to eliminate the entire Tutsi population. During this period, several devastating massacres of Tutsi civilians were carried out.

More than 400 Tutsi were killed in Kibirira, in Gisenyi Prefecture, in 1990. More than 1,500 Tutsi in the prefectures of Ruhengeri and Gisenyi were killed by government militia and the local Hutu population in 1991. In 1992 the Rwandan government instigated the murder of more than 300 civilian Tutsi in the Bugesera region of the Kigali Prefecture.

▼ EVENTS IN ▼
NEIGHBORING BURUNDI

In the 1980s the Tutsi ruler of Burundi promised to improve conditions for the Hutu in Burundi. However, Tutsi local authorities blocked these measures, resulting in a Hutu uprising that killed hundreds of Tutsi. To avenge this incident, the Tutsi army massacred approximately 20,000 Hutu.

Burundi held its first democratic elections in 1993. This led to the election of Burundi's first

During the genocide against Tutsi in Rwanda, this man was mistaken for a Tutsi and killed. Although he was a Hutu, because of his height he was assumed to be a Tutsi. This tragic example shows that the Hutu and Tutsi cannot be told apart solely on the basis of physical features.

Hutu president, Melchior Ndadaye. In October 1993 after only four months in office, Ndadaye was assassinated by the Tutsi-dominated military of Burundi. This led to Hutu attacks against local Tutsi. The ethnic strife that broke out left more than 50,000 people dead. More than half a million Hutu fled Burundi.

Hutu extremists in Rwanda demanded that their government send an army into neighboring Burundi to help the Hutu there fight the Tutsi military.

Tensions in the region were intensifying. African leaders hoped to find diplomatic ways of calming the violence. President Habyarimana of Rwanda and the new Hutu president of Burundi, Cyprien Ntaryamira, attended a regional meeting in Tanzania. On April 6, 1994, they returned together on Habyarimana's airplane. As they approached Kigali airport the airplane was shot down. Both Hutu presidents were killed.

▼ GENOCIDE ▼

The anger and confusion after the tragic death of the Hutu presidents allowed the Hutu extremists in Rwanda to seize power from the more moderate Hutu in Habyarimana's government. Immediately after the plane crash, Hutu extremists began to kill the Tutsi and moderate Hutu on their hit lists in Kigali. The killings soon spread throughout the country. The killings were carried out mostly by the president's force of guards and the armed militia known as Interahamwe, meaning those who attack together. The Interahamwe was controlled by the president's political party.

A new government of Hutu extremists was put in place by the Rwandan military. The extremists now controlled the national newspapers and both a national and a privately owned radio station. They used the media to urge the local population to kill their Tutsi neighbors and relatives and anyone who opposed the killings. The aim of the Hutu extremists was genocide, or the systematic killing of all people of a particular group, race, or political party.

Hutu extremists enforced a policy of genocide, believing that only the slaughter of the Tutsi population would bring about the final solution to the ethnic problems in Rwanda. More than half a million people, mostly Tutsis, were killed in Rwanda in three months.

Meanwhile, in neighboring Burundi, Hutu and Tutsi extremists continued to attack each other. Between 1993 and 1997, more than 150,000 have died.

▼ THE RPF VICTORY ▼

While the Hutu government of Rwanda concentrated on murdering the Tutsi population

Nearly one million Tutsis were murdered during the genocide in Rwanda, mostly by Hutu neighbors wielding machetes, or knives, such as those seen here. After the RPF took control of Rwanda, millions of Hutu fled, leaving behind their weapons.

and all government opponents, the RPF gained control of the countryside. By early July 1994, the RPF had taken over all of Rwanda, except for a small security zone in the southwest established by the French, who maintained close links with their former colony.

The defeated Hutu military forces and about 2 million Hutu refugees fled to Congo, Tanzania, and other neighboring countries. Several hundred Tutsi, who had been living in exile in those same countries for more than thirty years,

Since the first Tutsi refugees fled Rwanda in 1959, millions of Tutsi and Hutu have fled Rwanda and Burundi to escape ethnic violence. Refugees (above) faced desperate hardships, and countless thousands died of starvation and disease.

then returned to Rwanda. Most of them settled in cities, especially in Kigali, where they took over the property and businesses of the Hutu who had fled.

In November 1996, war in eastern Congo forced the majority of the Hutu refugees there to return to Rwanda. Many found that the property they had left behind had been taken over the Tutsi.

Rwanda now faces several difficult questions. How will the government solve the problem of property ownership? How will it bring to trial the more than 100,000 Hutu who have been arrested on charges of genocide? Also, the world is watching to see how the International Tribunal for Rwanda, based in Arusha, Tanzania, will punish those who planned and carried out the genocide against the Tutsi and the "moderate" Hutu.

The 1994 genocide against the Tutsi was among the worst crimes against humanity in recent history. For many years to come, the major problem facing the people of Rwanda will be how to deal psychologically with the brutal murder of nearly a million of their citizens.▲

6

THE FUTURE

AFTER THE 1994 GENOCIDE OF NEARLY A million Rwandans—mostly Tutsis—the biggest challenge that faces the new government is how to bring its people together. Many Tutsi suffered at the hands of extremist Hutu. Many survivors have lost their entire families. The persecution and violence have resulted in thousands of orphans, widows, and disabled persons. Many survivors bear scars of machetes, knives, and other lethal tools.

Besides the physical wounds, the psychological damage has been extreme. The majority of people witnessed killings or saw dead, mutilated bodies in their neighborhoods and on the streets. Moreover, thousands of women have given birth to children fathered by men who raped them and killed their family members. These children,

57

Hutu and Tutsi children from Rwanda and Burundi have witnessed shocking events. One of the challenges faced by their countries today is how to heal the psychological damage suffered by these young people.

called "children of shame," are often shunned
and tormented by society.

There are now more than 100,000 prisoners,
mostly Hutu, accused of taking part in the
killings. Human-rights observers think that as
many as 40 percent of those inmates may be
innocent. They may have been imprisoned simply
because they demanded the return of property
that is now occupied by Tutsi soldiers or their
families. The tendency to blame all Hutu for the
genocide in 1994 leads to great injustices.

These basic facts show how devastating the
damage has been for both groups. Reconciliation
between the Tutsi and the Hutu will be a very
difficult process. National reconciliation will
depend on justice being done where crimes have
been committed and on the willingness of people
to forgive one another. Nobody knows how long
it will take for people's anger to cool.

The Hutu believe that the present government
in Rwanda is dominated by the Tutsi minority.
The Rwandan army today is largely composed of
members of the RPF, which overthrew the Hutu
military government. Although the current
president and the prime minister of Rwanda are
Hutu, many Hutu complain that all the key
government positions are in the hands of Tutsi.
Many people say that the strongest person in
Rwanda today is the vice president and minister
of defense, Major General Paul Kagame. He is a

The future of both Hutu and Tutsi children depends on peace between the two groups.

Tutsi who left Rwanda with his family as a two-year-old after the Rwandan Revolution of 1959. Whoever rules Rwanda, one thing is clear—the survival of Rwanda depends on the cooperation between the Tutsi and the Hutu.▲

Glossary

abiru A group of advisers who kept the secrets of the Tutsi king.

colonization (in Africa) The actions that European countries took to take control of African countries against the will of Africans.

coup The overthrow of a government by a rebel group.

extremist One who favors radical political actions.

garagu Servant or vassal to a king or a lord.

genocide The intentional destruction of a racial, political, or ethnic group.

imandwa Spirits of dead heroes.

karinga The royal drum.

Kubandwa Ceremony that initiated young Hutu and Tutsi into adulthood.

refugee One who flees to a foreign country to escape persecution or other hardship.

shebuja Lord in the Rwandan feudal system.

ubuhake Rwandan feudal system. Under *ubuhake*, a person of lower status (a vassal, or *garagu*) worked for a person of higher status (a lord, or *shebuja*).

umupfumu A diviner, or one who can predict future events.

umwami The Tutsi king.

For Further Reading

Africa. San Diego, CA: Greenhaven Press, 1992.

Isaac, John. *Rwanda: Fierce Clashes in Central Africa.* 1st ed. Woodbridge, CT: Blackbirch Press, 1992.

Oliver, Roland, and J. D. Fage. *A Short History of Africa.* New York: Facts on File, 1988.

Twagilimana, Aimable. *Teenage Refugees from Rwanda Speak Out.* New York: The Rosen Publishing Group, 1997.

Watson, Catherine. *Exile from Rwanda: Background of an Invasion.* Washington, DC: U.S. Committee for Refugees, 1991.

Challenging Reading

Destexhe, Alain. *Rwanda and Genocide in the Twentieth Century.* Translated by Alison Marschner. New York: New York University Press, 1995.

Lemarchand, Rene. *Rwanda and Burundi.* New York/Washington/London: Praeger Publishers, 1970.

Index

A
ancestor worship, 30–32
art, 23–24

B
Bahutu Manifesto, 41–42
Bantu peoples, 11
baskets and pottery, 24
Belgium, 40–43
Burundi, 9
    conflict in, 11, 44, 46, 53, 59
    democratic elections of, 50, 52

C
cattle, 13, 15, 17–18, 19, 20, 24,
    30, 32, 38
Christianity, 29, 35–36, 41
Coup of Rucunshu (1896), 16

D
dancing, 24, 28
divination, 32–33
drums, 26–28

E
education, 35, 41, 46
European contact, 20, 24, 26, 37

F
farming, 11, 17, 30

G
garagu (vassal or servant), 18, 20,
    42
genocide, 35, 52–57, 59
Gikongoro Prefecture, 11, 44

H
Habyarimana, Major General, 46–
    48, 52

hunting, 11, 30

I
Imana (Supreme Being), 15, 26,
    29–30, 32–33
initiation ceremonies (Kubandwa),
    33–35
Interahamwe (militia), 53
International Tribunal for Rwanda,
    55–56

K
Kagame, Paul, 60
Kigali Prefecture, 11, 50, 52, 55
Kigeri V Ndahindurwa (Tutsi
    king), 43
king (umwami), role of, 14–16
Kinyarwanda (language), 9

L
land ownership, 20, 55, 59
literature, 23, 26

M
marriage, 18, 22, 26
milk, 19, 27, 31, 38
missionaries, 41
music, 26–28
Musinga (king of Rwanda), 16

N
Ndadaye, Melchior (president of
    Burundi), 52
Ntaryamira, Cyprien (president of
    Burundi), 52
Nyabingi, 26, 33–34
Nyanza, Rwanda, 42

P
poetry, 23–24, 26, 27

63

Q

queen mother (*umugabekazi*), 16

R

refugees, 11, 48, 55
RPF (Rwandan Patriotic Front), 48, 53–54, 59
Rutarindwa (king of Rwanda), 16
Rwanda, Kingdom of, 14–16, 37–38
Rwandan Revolution, 42–43, 48, 60
Ryangombe, 26, 33, 34

S

sacrifices, animal, 27, 31–32, 34
shebuja (lord or master), 18, 20, 23, 42

social structure, 17, 20, 27, 40
songs, 26, 31, 34
spirits, 26, 30, 34

T

Tanzania, 9, 11, 44, 46, 52, 55
Twa peoples, 9, 11, 14, 22, 27, 29–30, 33

U

ubuhake (feudal system), 18, 20, 41
Uganda, 9, 11, 33, 48

W

warriors (*intore*), 13, 20, 23–24, 26–28

ABOUT THE AUTHOR

Born in Butare, Rwanda, Aimable Twagilimana holds an M.A. in English from the National University of Rwanda and an M.A. in applied linguistics from the University of Reading, England. He received his Ph.D. in American Literature from the State University of New York at Buffalo, where he was a Fulbright scholar. Currently professor of English at the State University College at Buffalo (Buffalo State College), he previously taught linguistics and literature at the National University of Rwanda. He has published many articles and books on Rwanda.

PHOTO CREDITS

Cover, pp. 13, 14 (R. Vargas), 17, 31, 47 © International Stock; pp. 8 and 28 © Viesti Associates, M. Jelliffe; p. 12 © Lauralea Gilpin; pp. 19, 51 © Aimable Twagilimana; pp. 21 (Dave Bartruff), 54 (David Turnley), 55, 58, and 60 (all Howard Davies) © Corbis; p. 25 after P. Marcel Pauwels, *Les Métiers et les Objets en Usage du Rwanda* (1953); pp. 39, 41, 45, 49 © AP Wide World Photos.

CONSULTING EDITOR AND LAYOUT

Gary N. van Wyk, Ph.D.

SERIES DESIGN

Kim Sonsky

PHOTO RESEARCH

Beatrice R. Grabish